Price Waterhouse Sectional

Santa Fe   1989

NEW MEXICO

NEW MEXICO

PHOTOGRAPHY • DAVID MUENCH

TEXT • TONY HILLERMAN

GRAPHIC ARTS CENTER PUBLISHING COMPANY

PORTLAND, OREGON

July thunderhead, Rio Grande River Valley at Las Cruces.

NEW
MEXICO

International Standard Book Number 0-912856-14-9

Library of Congress Catalog Number 74-75125

Copyright © MCMLXXIV by Graphic Arts Center Publishing Company

P.O. Box 10306 • Portland, Oregon 97210 • 503/226-2402

Designer • Bonnie Muench

Typography • Paul O. Giesey/Adcrafters

Printer • Graphic Arts Center

Binding • Lincoln & Allen

Printed in the United States of America

Ninth Printing

King's Palace, Carlsbad Caverns National Park.

Living forms of Taos Pueblo. Following pages: Summer skies over Shiprock in Navajo country.

Ancient Keres Pueblo of Acoma, in its lofty setting between
sky expanse and Desert plain. The oldest continuously
occupied settlement in the United States. Left: Ripples in
time, White Sands National Monument.

Pueblo women carry ollas at annual Gallup Indian
Ceremonial. Right: Thunderhead explodes into summer
skies above Laguna Pueblo and 11,389 foot Mt. Taylor.

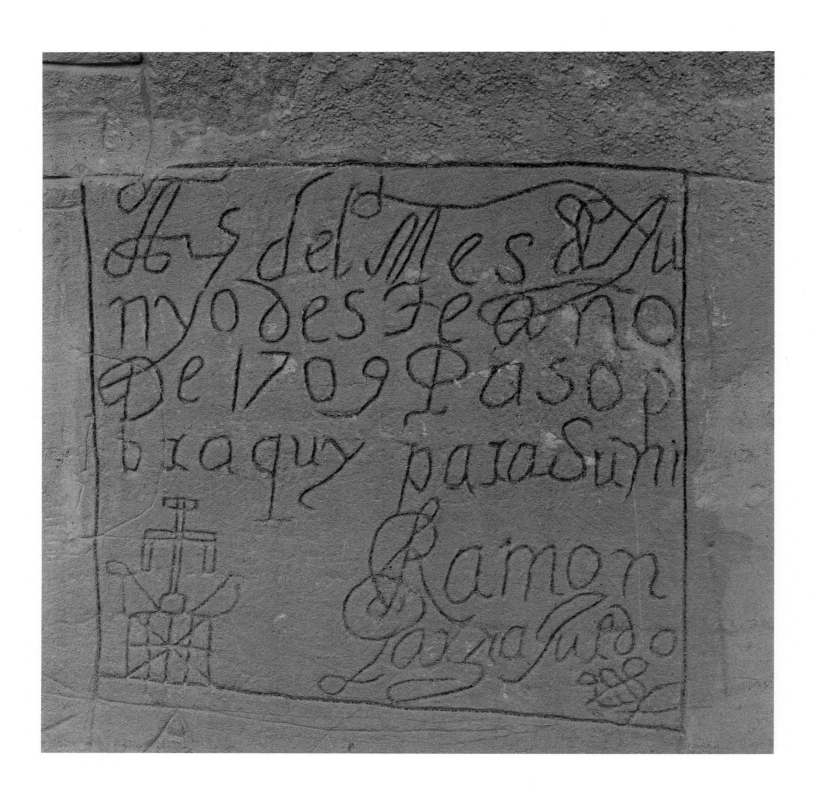

El Morro National Monument, Ramon Garcia Jurado
1709 inscription. Right: After Coronado passed this way
in 1540, hundreds of Spanish soldiers and priests
left their names and notations in sandstone.

Summer rains cast a profusion of sunflowers in the
dry desert plains. Left: Timeless avenue of Pueblo adobe
and ladders, "sky city" of Acoma.

Ta-ay-a llona, sacred mountain to the Zuni.
Left: Old Zuni, hand polished, turquoise necklace
acquired by Millicent Rogers. Now displayed at
Millicent Rogers Memorial Museum in Taos.

Spanish bayonet, or narrow-leafed yucca, lends
spring beauty to the austerity of a thirsting land.

Above: Sandstone pinnacles in Zuni mountains.
Below: Zuni animal-figures design on plate.

Winter's sometimes gentle sometimes harsh interlude.
Navajo horses romp in a sea of white. Left: Striking mural
adorns church at Santo Domingo Pueblo.

Enduring beauty of the Desert. A lone bloom of Prickly
pear cactus. Left: In foreboding contrast a timeless mood
surrounds the volcanic spire of Shiprock.

Navajo woman tends a watchful eye on her sheep
through a January blizzard. Left: A highly complex design,
Two Gray Hills rug composition woven by Julia Jumbo.

Everything has a season. Traditional Navajo winds his
way home from the trading post. Left: Swollen flow of
mud and silt testify to the violence of a summer's
flash flood below Mesa Gigante, Valencia County.

New Mexico's skies emphatically determine the earth.
With scant moisture from Pacific and Gulf, and country
above 3000 feet elevation, the sun's glare seres the land,
Table Mesa. Right: Tumbleweed design, Cooks Range.

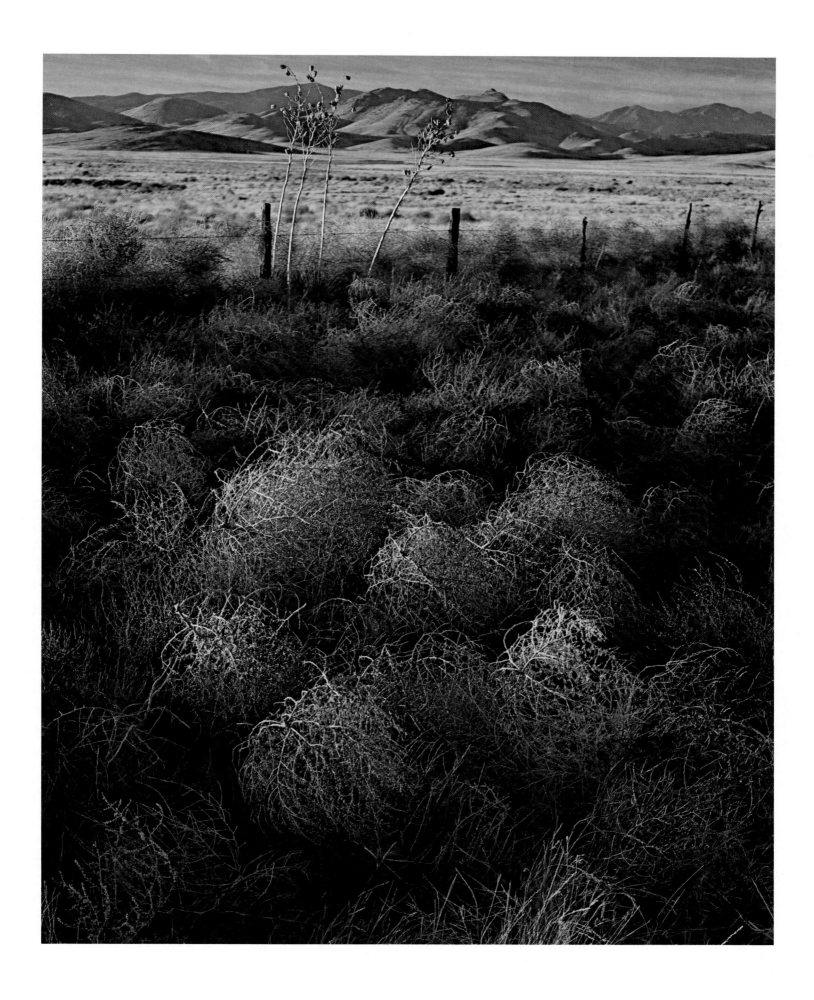

NEW
MEXICO

Often it begins in the late afternoon. A great bank of fog builds along the ridges of the Sandia Mountains, forming an opaque wall. It looms eventually a thousand feet higher than the 10-thousand foot crest. Then it begins to spill—like the heavy vapor from a beaker of acid rolling down the glass.

From Albuquerque's West Mesa residential districts across the Rio Grande one sees it in perspective—a niagara of fog pouring slowly down the cliffs of the mountain range. But for those who live on Albuquerque's northeastern fringes, in the Sandia foothills, this spectacle takes place almost directly overhead. The cataract of mist falls silently toward their roofs as if some great aerial dam had broken to pour down the clouds. The fog rarely reaches the foothills. Somewhere up the slope the warm air on the west face of the mountain reaches a balance with the cold mist pressing downward. The cloud begins to evaporate, ravelling away from the bottom. Then the red light of sunset catches all this and turns it pink. And what had been awe-inspiring is reduced to mere beauty.

This eye-catching phenomenon warns the central Rio Grande Valley—where almost half of New Mexico's people live—that the weather is changing. The Great Plains air mass east of the Sandia and Manzano Mountains has become colder (or warmer) than the Colorado Plateau air west of the mountains. Two of the edges which meet in New Mexico are rubbing together.

It seems to those of us who live in New Mexico and try to understand her that many edges meet in this most peculiar of the 50 states. In meeting they give her climate, landscape and society its character. It is here that the Rocky Mountains finally end in a chaos of parallel ridges. Here the Great Plains lap at last against the edge of these mountains. And here the Sonoran Desert—spread over an immensity of Mexico—is finally overcome by too much altitude and too many late summer thunderstorms. No other state offers such an abrupt contrast in landscape. Six of the continent's seven biological life zones are found within her borders—ranging down from the cold and windy arctic-alpine country above timberline to the sometimes torrid Lower Sonoran Desert.

New Mexico also lies under the edges of the forces which shape the American climate. It is too far west to get more than the weak fringe of the wet Gulf Stream air, and too many mountain ranges east to feel full effects of the Pacific Westerlies, and on the very boundary of those great arctic blizzards which bulge down out of Canada across the nation's midlands. The net effect of location and altitude is a sort of cancellation—a climate basically dry, mild and dominated by the sun. The thin, dry air moderates the summer's heat and almost constant sunlight warms the winters.

Something like this might also be said about its culture. Its population, too, has been formed by edges and over-lappings—the meetings of migrations which had lost their force with cultures which had lost their intolerance.

We know little of the first who came—only that they were passing through on a southward migration away from the glaciers and toward the sun. A few remained and became the cultures we call the Cochise, and the Mogollon, and the Mimbres. From them came the Anasazi—the Old Ones—who built great apartment-style pueblos, and made beautiful pottery and formidable magic and provided the roots of the first sophisticated civilization in what would become the United States. Around this peaceful communal pueblo civilization lapped the exhausted edges of later migrations.

The Athabascans came at the tag end of their long struggle down from the north—they were still strong enough to harass these peaceful farmers but too weak to overwhelm them. And so the Athabascans stayed, and learned and became the Navajos and the Apaches. The next wave were the Spanish—the last spasm of expansion of a dying empire. Had the Spanish arrived a little earlier, the peaceful culture of farmers would likely have been erased even more thoroughly than was that of the mighty Aztec. But these were milder conquistadores, representing a worn-out empire softened by internal decay and by the spreading philosophy of a Saint called Francis of Assisi. Finally all of this was engulfed by the westward sweep of the Anglo-Americans. But without the magnet of material wealth to attract it, even Manifest Destiny lost force and ferocity here and allowed other cultures to survive. For once, the American melting pot failed to operate. New Mexico produced a mosaic of cultures instead of a mixture.

Always, as far back as geologists can read earth's history in its rocks, what is now New Mexico had been a place of margins and meetings. Here, a billion-and-a-half years ago, the lifeless Precambrian Ocean washed against the headlands of the still dead continent. Its ebb and flow built layers of iron-rich silt which now streak the western cliffs of Caballo Mountain and the eastern escarpment of the San Andres Range. Down through the eons, as the planet aged and its oceans rose and fell with the shifting crust, fate made this the pattern for what would be New Mexico. The Ordovician Ocean made it an island and left behind immense deposits of limestone. The Silurian Sea, swarming with huge water scorpions and primitive fishes, lapped across its beaches and laid down layers of fossil-rich dolomite. In the Devonian era New Mexico was again on the margin of land and ocean—an immense steaming lowland of fern forests. On its fringes the coral grew and died and now forms the great bioherm mounds (some up to 350 feet high) in the Sacramento Mountains. The Mississippian and Pennsylvanian periods came, and produced coal and oil, and then the Permian. Southern New Mexico sank under a great inland sea surrounded by incredible barrier reefs. Geologists call these reefs the Capitan and Goat Seep. From them, in subsequent millions of years, percolating water would dissolve away the world's largest subsurface cavities which we call the Carlsbad Caverns. Later, perhaps 200 million years ago, the ocean gate closed and what had been open water became an inland sea. It stretched from Santa Fe southward over much of southeastern New Mexico

—teeming with marine life, alternately drying under the searing sun and flooding with the changing climate. Gradually the land rose, draining the ocean southeastward until only the extreme southeastern corner of the state remained under the sea. The age of Dinosaurs came, bringing to New Mexico principally the amphibian reptiles—the 85 foot long, 50-ton Brachiosaurus, the ponderous Stegosaurus and a dazzling variety of others, which left their bones to be quarried in truck loads from the cliffs of Rio Arriba County.

New Mexico's landscape began taking its modern shape in what geologists call the Laramide Revolution—that paroxysm which shook the earth about 25 million years ago. New Mexico rose above sea level to stay tilted as it is today, from northwest to southwest. Southwestern New Mexico spouted and boiled with volcanoes building the Mogollon plateau. To the east, volcanic eruptions pushed Sierra Blanca 12,000 feet into the sky. Mount Taylor, the Turquoise Mountain of the Navajos, was formed by another of these Neogene eruptions, as was Shiprock and most of the similar volcanic necks which dot the state's western half. In the south, the Tularosa Arch collapsed in one of nature's major cataclysms. A highland the size of Connecticut sank almost a mile, converting a mountain massif into a hundred-mile-long depression. The mountain ranges which rims it now once were its foothills. Very late in this period of recurrent volcanism—perhaps a mere million years ago—the earth produced a spectacle which gives New Mexico one of its most unusual features—the Valle Grande Caldera.

Eons of volcanic activity had formed the Jemez Mountains along the western edge of the Rio Grande trough. And over this mountain range towered what some geologists believe must have been the largest volcanic peak on the continent. (Some guess it was as tall as 25,000 feet.) The same forces which built soon destroyed it.

The first explosions opened vents on the northeastern face of the mountain—blasting millions of tons of melted rock miles into the air and spreading a layer of ashes as far north and east as Oklahoma and Kansas. Then another hole opened on the east side of the volcano from which gushed an ash flood up to 250 feet deep. What was left of the mountain then destroyed itself. Other eruptions spread a blanket of burned rock up to 1,000 feet deep over the surrounding plateau. With an estimated 25 cubic miles of its insides spewed into the atmosphere, the volcano collapsed into itself. What had been one of the greatest peaks in the hemisphere sank into a cavity 12 miles in diameter and as much as 3500 feet deep. (The eruption of Krakatoa Volcano, the largest explosion recorded by man on this planet, left a crater four miles across and 2000 feet deep.) Geologists say this caldera rivals one in Siberia as the largest on earth. It is now a great bowl of grass, a rancher's summer pasture.

If one stands in the fir-aspen forests which rims this bowl the cattle which graze far below seem smaller than natural —out of scale with a setting. The bowl is simply too large

for the eye to credit and this odd optical effect is heightened by the transparent high-altitude air which robs the scene of the proper sense of dim blue distance.

It is, in fact, this thin, dry, clear air which gives New Mexico and Southern Rocky Mountain highlands much of their unusual visual character. Passengers on west-bound flights over the state can hardly fail to notice the phenomena. The Great American midlands they have crossed have been, in most seasons, at least partially hidden by an opaque layer of clouds. What landscape is open to view is made dim and hazy by a layer of low altitude air which is heavy with humidity. This layer of haze thins as the land rises to become the "High Plains" of Texas. Across the New Mexico border, the land gains altitude steadily emerging from this hazy layer like the headland of a continent rising from a shelving sea. The dimness is gone, the softness, the haze. Ahead, to the north and to the south, the mountains are stark outlines in the harsh, clear light, their eastern slopes still packed with the winter's snow. The air is no longer translucent. It is transparent.

Part of this effect, of course, is a matter of moisture. Or lack of it. Albuquerque will average only 8 inches of rain a year (compared with 34 inches at Dallas, and Kansas City and Cleveland, and 44 at Charleston, Norfolk, Tacoma, Wilmington and Baltimore, and 68 at Mobile). But much of it is altitude. The troposphere loses 1/30th of its density with each 900 feet of altitude gained. New Mexico has been lifted an average of 5700 feet above the oceans which once lapped across it. Its lowest point (in the extreme southwestern corner of the state) is a thousand feet higher than the loftiest peak in the Missouri Ozarks. One who gazes from the campus of St. John's College at Santa Fe across the Rio Grande Valley toward Los Alamos looks through air which has lost a fourth of its weight. It is low in oxygen, low in carbon dioxide and high in hydrogen. It offers little to defract or diffuse the light. Thus the white buildings of the Los Alamos Scientific Laboratory, more than 30 miles away, are etched sharply against the dark green background of ponderosa pines. Thus the lights of a New Mexico city seen from a distance are robbed of the soft and charming glow that belong to humid lands. Instead they are a hundred thousand pinpoints of brilliance etched in the darkness. Here, the eye trained to milder light is deceived by distances, by horizons which stretch away 150 miles. Citizens of this arid tableland find themselves oppressed by lower climates. The low country sky closes them in, and gives them something like claustrophobia, and makes them yearn for the mountains.

Except for that strip of "Little Texas" oil country on the extreme southeastern margin of New Mexico no part of the state is without its mountains. They range from the Animas to the Zunis—from the Bears, Big Burros and the Broke Offs, to the Victorios, Tularosas and Tres Hermanos—in all, 73 ranges and 310 peaks are found worthy of naming on the better maps. Seven of the summits tower more than 13,000 feet above sea level, and 85 are at least two miles high. Most of them are arranged in ragged, north-south ridges, dominated by their own long exhausted volcanic peaks, and dominating, in turn, the valleys into which their snowpack drains. On the average, they are less massive than the Northern Rockies, somewhat lower, older, with part of the rawness eroded away by eons of time and weather.

In the north, they bulge down across the Colorado border, rising from the high tableland of the Colorado Plateau. The greatest range is the Sangre de Cristo, named by the Spanish for the Blood of Christ because the peaks turn red at sunset. These wall off the upper Rio Grande valley on the east. West of the river the rampart is formed by the ancient Nacimientos and the Jemez Range. Beyond them to the west lie the Ceboletas and the Chuskas. To New Mexicans, these form the "Northern Mountains." In general, they are higher and the snow remains in sheltered east-slope notches until the very end of summer.

The Southern Mountains are lower principally because they rise from a lower base. Here their feet are planted in the desert—the Tularosa Basin or the Plains of San Agustin. While they tower as much as a mile above surrounding terrain the net altitude is less and so is the amount of moisture they collect.

More than any other feature, it is the ubiquitous mountains that influence life in New Mexico. They collect nearly all the state's scanty moisture—building up snowpacks from October through May and releasing it through the summer to fill irrigation ditches down in the valleys of the Rio Grande, and the Pecos, and the San Juan. On late summer afternoons, warm updrafts build towers of clouds miles into the sky over their high ridges. These thunderheads produce their pyrotechnic lightning (and a measles rash of forest fires) and drift eastward, trailing brief, noisy rainshowers over the valleys. From Santa Fe, one can sometimes see as many as five such thundershowers simultaneously—one rumbling over the Sangre de Cristos, one obscuring Los Alamos and the Jemez Range with sheets of rain, another forming an immense pile of white a hundred miles away over Mount Taylor, and the others trailing curtains of thundershower over the Manzanos and across these rugged little outcroppings which New Mexicans call—with bilingual redundancy—"the Cerrillos Hills." Indians of the Rio Grande Pueblos call these displays "male rains" in ironic reference to their high ratio of noise, and visual display to the low level of moisture produced. "Female rains" are the much rarer general storms which bless the state now and then with fruitful, quiet, gentle precipitation. It's not unusual to have three drift across Albuquerque on a single (and generally sunny) afternoon, leaving narrow strips of the city drenched but most of it still totally dry. The storms are products of mountain updrafts, which push the thin air too high in the stratosphere to hold its moisture.

In early mornings, the same mountains produce downdrafts which bring air from the forests, and the meadows down into the streets of town. Early risers smell the scent of pine resin, and blue lupine, and nameless wild things. In New Mexico, the mountains affect the climate of the valleys, and the climate of the soul.

A scant one million people live in New Mexico which is the fifth largest state. Its 121,666 square miles equal the combined land area of Maine, New Hampshire, Vermont, Massachusetts, Rhode Island, Connecticut, New York, New Jersey, Maryland and Delaware. The population, if spread evenly, would average out to a bit more than eight people per square mile (the national average is 58 per mile). But people can live only where there is water. Thus, this million live clustered in a sort of oasis civilization—leaving most of the country almost totally empty.

Approximately a third of New Mexico's citizens occupy the 400 square miles of Greater Albuquerque and its environs. More than half live in a narrow irrigated belt down the Rio Grande. The remainder are clustered mostly in the northwestern and southwestern corners, where petroleum industries have flourished and where the Pecos and San Juan rivers pump irrigation water and provide enough moisture for a small farming industry. The "section line" pattern of the American farm belt, which divides the land into tidy mile-square places each with its households, is made impossible here by the arid climate.

Those who value such misanthropic favors find that New Mexico can still bestow, the gift of isolation. It is still easy to be alone. Even from the very heart of the state's major population center—Albuquerque's Northeast Heights shopping district—the pressures of civilization are eased by the knowledge that escape is near. From the noisy traffic jam at Menaul and Louisiana Boulevard, it's only minutes away to the immense grassy emptiness of the West Mesa, or the spruce and aspen forests of the Sandias, or the shady cottonwood bosques of the Rio Grande bottoms —each offering its own variety of silence.

The first men to come were hunters. Their ancestors had come from Asia, following the mastadon and musk ox over what was then a land bridge from Siberia. They had drifted southward, escaping the ice, following the migration routes of the now-extinct mammals on which they preyed. And, being nomads, they left little more trace of their passing than did the dire wolves and the saber-tooth cats which hunted with them. Of their early interglacial migration a clear-cut trace of only one camp has been found.

Crude stone tools, a roughly shaped lance tip, and the cooked bones of ice age animals were left on the floor of Sandia Cave. Torrential rains of the glacial periods leached ochre out of cliff and covered these remains with a thick yellow deposit. This, and the fact that the hunter had been toasting the bones of the long-vanished North American horse, camel and giant ground sloth, have caused his presence to be dated back as early as 25,000 years. Until something earlier is found, this Sandia Man is called the First American.

We know almost nothing about him. The mouth of the cave he chose—a deep hole high on the wall of Las Huertas Canyon on the northeast slope of Sandia Mountain—commands a breathtaking view. One can see down-canyon all the way across the Rio Grande Valley to the Jemez Range. And across the canyon, there's the great forested slope of Sandia Mountain with puffy summer clouds dragging their bottoms through the spruce at its crest. This might suggest an appreciation of beauty. But perhaps he was driven here by danger. Neither the wolves nor the saber-tooth cats could reach this lofty perch.

Those who came later left more tracks to read. A large band of hunters trapped a family of mammoths in a bog near Clovis, on New Mexico's eastern plains, and left a tell-tale wealth of broken weapons and worn butchering tools among the bones. Anthropologists called them Clovis Man and dated them some 13,000 years before present. Their hunting methods, their large leaf-shaped lance points, and stone working techniques have since been detected at Ice Age kill sites up and down the east slope of the Rockies. After Clovis Man came Folsom, who stampeded a herd of long-horned bison into a swamp near the village of Folsom, New Mexico, and killed 13 of them, and left amid their bones the thin, fluted, "Folsom Points" which represent Stone Age America's most beautiful weaponry. This Folsom culture survived until perhaps 9,000 years ago, leaving scores of hunting camps buried under the gramma grass on the plains which overlook the Rio Grande Valley. After him came other hunters, killing with larger, cruder lance points. Finally, civilization began.

Civilization seems to have begun about the same time on the western side of the Mogollon Plateau where southern New Mexico joins Arizona, and on the Colorado Plateau in the barren "Four Corners" where Colorado, Utah, Arizona and New Mexico touch. The hunters had become foragers, gatherers of seeds, makers of baskets in which to store and carry foods. The highly portable skin shelters in which Folsom Man lived gave way to permanent pit houses as the nomad became farmer, planting domesticated seeds and harvesting corn and squash. By the time of Christ, the Hohokam people had developed effective irrigation systems on the Gila and Mimbres Rivers in southwestern New Mexico and the Anasazi were diverting arroyo floods with sophisticated damming systems into corn fields of northwestern New Mexico. From their pit houses they moved above ground, devising building techniques which used cut stones and puddled adobe, they also developed an art for ceramics, weaving, pictographs and petroglyphs.

The cultures which developed from these roots were rich and varied. They prospered in the period when Europe groaned through the bloody autocratic chaos of the Dark Ages and they flowered into what the cultural historians call the Golden Age of the Pueblos. New Mexico, plus Colorado and Arizona where they adjoin its northwestern borders, are dotted with literally thousands of ruins left by these people—most of them still unexcavated.

By early in the 12th Century, Pueblo Bonito in Chaco Canyon had been built into a five-story stone apartment complex of 800 rooms and a three acre floor plan. Some 5,000 persons lived in this community, their religious and medicine clans using 32 ceremonial kivas, and their farm lands watered by an extensive system of arroyo dams. Other such centers flourished in Frijoles Canyon just be-

low the modern site of Los Alamos, at Mesa Verde, and elsewhere.

These pueblo-dwellers evolved a sophisticated cultural system based on trade, assigned duties, and social responsibilities. They developed art—music and dance as well as visual. They devised a form of government which came closer to modern democratic ideals than did the Athens of Pericles. Most important of all, they developed a philosophy which survives into the 20th Century and is part of the flavor of modern New Mexico.

While European and middle Eastern civilization saw man as lord of the universe, the center of nature, the reason for all creation, the Pueblo philosophers saw themselves and their brothers as parts of nature. Their happiness and well-being depended upon remaining in harmony with birds and beasts, sky and stone. Duty, health and fulfillment lay —not in the egocentric European concept of personal ambition, individual attainment and material acquisition, but in such values as generosity, brotherhood and the proper performance of the role to which one's clan, kiva and pueblo had assigned him. There has never been a civilization quite like it. It was free, hospitable, and peaceful. In the face of what was coming it was, quite literally, too good to last. Yet, in many ways it did last. It survives today in the 19 Pueblos of modern New Mexico—and in the influence it has had on the successive migrations which were to lap around it.

The next to come were the Athabascans—the people who would become the Navajos and the Apaches of the Southwest, and the Iroquois of Canada and the Eastern woodlands, and the complex fishing civilizations of the Pacific Northwest. But as was its pattern, New Mexico was on the fringe of this human wave. Only a trickle reached the Southern Rockies—little bands of stragglers who lived hungrily off the land. We guess at most of what happened. They raided the peaceful Pueblo communities, and stole from them, and were awed by their civilization, and by the magic of these people who could, with their prayer plumes and their ritual dances, call the clouds across the sky, and make rain fall. Most of these newcomers learned to plant and harvest, ended their wanderings and became the Navajos, calling themselves Diné, "The People," and their cousins, who rejected the sedentary life, Apaches. In Navajo, the word means "enemy."

Perhaps the arrival of the Athabascans ended the Golden Age of Pueblo building. Most likely it was many things. We know that the people who now occupy Cochiti Pueblo made several of their community's six moves during this period. We know that after abandoning their great pueblo of Tyuonyi in Frijoles Canyon, most of their new townsites were chosen for defense. But we also know a story tree rings have to tell us. In the summer of 1276 the magic of the kivas began to fail. The clouds no longer came at the call of the ritual dancers. The drought lasted unbroken for 24 consecutive years. There's been nothing like it since. And when it was ended, only the blowing dust moved in the last of the great peublos of the Golden Age. The

drought, perhaps augmented by diseases, seems to have pretty well depopulated New Mexico. The survivors rebuilt their communities along the Rio Grande, and in the valley of the Pecos, and the Jemez, and at other lower sites where there was living water. And thus it remained until the edge of the next great human tide washed feebly into New Mexico from the South.

Had the invasion happened two or three generations earlier, it's not likely that the gentle Pueblo culture would have survived. But the little column of 130 soldiers, a few score families, and 83 ox carts of supplies which Don Juan de Oñate brought north from Chihuahua in 1598 was not the same sort of invasion that destroyed the Aztec empire, or tumbled the mighty Inca war machine into ruins. Oñate was not Cortéz, nor Pizarro, and the Spain of Philip II was very different than the Spain of Charles I.

The tide of the Spanish Empire was at flood, but the force was gone. Oñate's ramshackle little column winding northward from the Rio Grande ford at El Paso del Norte, was part of the final spasm of expansion. Ten years earlier Queen Elizabeth's new fleet had destroyed the antiquated and outgunned Spanish navy in the English Channel and left the Duke of Alba's invincible army stranded in the Netherlands. The balance of power had shifted, but in terms of New Mexico history, it was more important that Philosophy had softened the fanaticism of the Conquistadores. Whatever mystical urge had inspired the incredible, ruthless destroying bravery of the conquests of Mexico and Peru had been infected. The Roman Catholic theologians had argued that American Indians were fellow humans, Children of God, endowed with an immortal soul, and had caused the Spanish Crown to accept that position, and decree that these pagans should be brought to Christianity—and not exterminated.

An older fashioned conquistador, Francisco Vasquez de Coronado, had explored the territory a half-century earlier, pursuing a myth of El Dorado, an Indian ruler who coated himself with gold, and the Seven Cities of Cibola, where gold was used as paving blocks. He had found, instead, the seven stone towns of Zuni, the Rio Grande civilization, and the emptiness of the Great Plains.

Coronado came for gold. Oñate's followers came to stay. They brought plows, seeds, sheep and axes, but few wives. Long exposure to the Moorish-Arabic culture had left them without Northern Europe's racial bigotry. They would find wives among the Indians.

Looking at this tiny column through the perspective of history helps one understand why the Indian cultures in its path survived while those of Eastern America did not. The English brought with them the concept of racial superiority and the metaphysics of Puritanism, Calvinism and the idea of "salvation of the elect and damnation of the many." Among the English and the Dutch there were no niggling, time wasting doubts and arguments about the Indians. Unless they got in the way, they were let alone. If the white man wanted their land, they were driven out or exterminated, with neither malice nor intended cruelty.

Lord Amherst, representing the British Crown in the English colonies, suggested that smallpox be spread among the savages to clear the land for more rapid development by the Christians, but germ warfare had not yet been perfected and nothing came of the idea. The English colonists moved slowly and left no Indian cultures behind them. They would have found the expedition of Oñate hard to understand.

These Spanish marched, literally, under two flags—the Royal Pennant of the Spanish Crown and the banner of the Catholic Church. They pledged loyalty to "the two majesties—God and Emperor." Oñate was a soldier, but he was surrounded by seven members of the Order of Friars Minor —followers of St. Francis who preached the joy of poverty and the brotherhood of man. The column's military purpose was to found and protect a colony which would hold the territory for the king, but these Franciscans sought a harvest of Indian souls baptised in the name of Christ. And how could one preach the message of conversion to Indians if the Army drove them away? And how could the government enslave them after they had been made Brothers-in-Christ? After the great Oñate died, this dichotomy of purpose would produce a crippling, century-long quarrel between church and state in New Mexico. But from the very beginning, it caused a special relationship between the Spanish and the dwellers of the pueblos.

Legend tells us Oñate's column exhausted its supplies south of Socorro in a strip of desert which maps still call Jornada del Muerto (Deadman's route). The legend reports that the Indian pueblo upriver sent runners with baskets of corn to rescue the invaders. Historians haven't confirmed this tale, but it fits with the pueblo tradition of generous hospitality. Whether or not this gesture was made, the Pueblos generally accepted the Spanish and were willing to hear about Christianity. Oñate met with leaders of more than 30 pueblos at what is now Santo Domingo and received their allegiance to Spain. Then he moved upstream to the confluence of Rio Chama with the Rio Grande. He named this pueblo San Juan of the Gentlemen in recognition of its hospitality and made it New Mexico's first capitol.

There was only a little fighting in this period in which New Mexico's Pueblo Indian culture became Spanish Pueblo. But it produced an epic feat of arms as awe-inspiring as the stand of Leonidas and his Spartan at Thermopylae. To appreciate the courage involved, you must see Acoma. And when you see it, it is almost impossible to believe this "sky city" fortress could have been stormed.

Acoma is a rock-and-adobe pueblo built atop an island of stone which juts 357 feet into the sky in the mesa country west of Albuquerque. Its top is irregular but almost level, 70 acres in size. A road has now been cut up its side, but in 1599, the only way to the top was via foot and handholds cut into the cliffs. Originally, the Acomans had accepted the Spanish. But when Lieutenant Juan de Zaldívar paused there with a dozen men en route on a journey of explorations, they were invited up the cliffs and ambushed.

Five of the thirteen fought their way to the edge of the precipice and jumped. Four somehow survived to take the tale of treachery to Oñate. A month later, Vicente de Zaldívar, the surviving 19-year-old brother of Juan, arrived with a punitive force of 70 men—more than half of the survivors of Oñate's army. Young Zaldívar left a dozen men to guard his horses and supplies and with the rest, fought his way, for three bloody days, up those cliffs, held by a mixed force of perhaps 1,000 Acoma and Zuni warriors. Historian-Anthropologist Charles Lummis, after examining the battleground, wrote this:

"The forcing of that awful cliff, the three days' death struggle hand-to-hand, the storm of that fortress town room by savage room—time records nothing more desperately brilliant."

By 1628, when Oñate died, Spanish control was firmly established in the Rio Grande Valley and the mountains which overlook it. The capitol was moved to Santa Fe in 1610, and mission churches were established in the various pueblos. The Pueblo Indians found the concepts of Christianity easy to adapt to their values of peace, brotherhood, and hospitality, and to their metaphysics of life-after-death, and a single all-powerful Creator, with benevolent interest in man. Even the "community of saints" concept of the Catholics was paralleled by their own idea of kachinas—the helpful ancestor spirits.

But the Spanish fought among themselves. The issues were old—the status of the Indians, and the conflict between church and state. It erupted repeatedly, with Governors excommunicated as heretics and Franciscan missionaries jailed as criminal traitors. The Pueblo Indians eyed this dispute, suffering its effects. In 1680 they decided to throw out the white man and return to their old ways.

The revolt seems to have been planned largely in the Taos Pueblo—which even today is one of the more conservative. Its instigator was Popé, who tradition tells us had been forced to work in a Spanish mine near Cerrillos. Only Isleta just south of Albuquerque and the Piro "salt" Pueblos in the Manzano Mountains remained loyal to the Spanish. The rebels struck on the night of August 10, wiping out the Spanish in many of the outlying settlements in a single bloody night. The survivors were besieged in the Palace of the Governors in Santa Fe—the thick-walled building which still forms one side of Santa Fe's central plaza. With their water supply exhausted, the colonists fought their way southward and, with aid from Isleta and Piro, reached El Paso. By year-end, the Indians were again masters of New Mexico.

The shaky Pueblo coalition quickly collapsed under the weight of Indian differences. The Spanish returned in 1692, under Don Diego de Vargas. Quickly and with little fighting, he restored Spanish control. (But the larger, better armed, force of De Vargas couldn't repeat young Zaldívar's conquest of Acoma. The Acomans held their fortress in the sky, then chose to accept Spanish control a year later.)

The story of the next 150 years for this northernmost of the Spanish colonies is one of poverty, government mis-management and neglect, and sporadic combat between the Spanish and their Pueblo Indian allies on one hand, and Navajo, Apache and Comanche-Kiowa war parties on the other.

With the decline of Spain as a world power, its colonial administration rotted. This ultimate colony on the extreme northern frontier was virtually forgotten. It depended on a supply line which stretched more than 2000 miles from Mexico City. Its colonists had virtually no source of money to buy manufactured goods or weapons. Spanish (and later Mexican) policy restricted firearms to the military—and even the military was most often armed only with lance and bow. In the face of this weakness, an event of historic importance was taking place. The horse, imported by the Spanish, had been discovered by the Plains Indians, the Navajo and the Apache. A bloody new dimension was added to the struggle for the frontier. Through the 18th Century the Spanish Pueblo civilization fought grimly for survival. Missions and pueblos and haciendas were abandoned. The Navajo pressed in from the northwest, the Apache from the south, and Comanche from the east. Colonial militiamen, often armed only with lances and bows, fought cavalry battles with Comanches armed with French-manufactured muskets. Population declined. Isolation increased. The fall of Spain to Napoleon was hardly noticed here. So far as Santa Fe was concerned, the Mexican war of independence did little more than change flags over the Palace of the Governors. The bad situation became worse as the new Republic of Mexico tore itself apart with internal strife. Then from the East another wave of migration began to trickle toward the Southern Rocky Mountains.

Some historians believe that had not the Santa Fe Trail, which opened in 1821, given New Mexico an alternate supply line during this period, the colony and its Spanish-Pueblo civilization would have been erased by the raiding tribes. It seems equally likely that had New Mexico offered more material wealth, the forces of American "Manifest Destiny" would have crushed the existing cultures as thoroughly as they did in California and Texas. But once again New Mexico was on the margin.

Anglo-Americans had trickled into the territory early in the 19th century, drifting down from the Northern Rockies to trap beaver and do illegal trading. When the Santa Fe Trail brought regular wagon trains from Missouri, the trickle increased. The Mexican government, nervous about the intentions of its giant neighbor, officially prohibited admission of these trader-adventurers. Unofficially the colony welcomed them for breaking the strangling monopoly held by Chihuahuan merchants on trade. When the Mexican War flared in 1846, the northern territory fell, virtually without resistance, into American hands.

The Treaty of Guadalupe Hidalgo and the subsequent Gadsden Purchase ceded all of what is now New Mexico to the United States. But here the traditional Anglo-American pattern of sweeping existing cultures away in the path of its westward march did not operate. There seemed to be almost nothing in this new territory which anyone wanted —a marginal farming economy principally operated by the Pueblo Indians, and a marginal cattle-sheep industry operated largely by the Spanish, a civilization of adobe villages scattered up the Rio Grande and its mountains, and a relentless and savage war with the nomadic Indians. There were at least two serious proposals that the United States should withdraw from this area and leave it to work out its own destiny. But the United States remained in authority and a third culture gradually superimposed itself over the Indian and Spanish.

There were two brief revolts, at Taos and Mora, both put down by U.S. Army artillery fire. (The Taos Indians took refuge in their mission church and were slaughtered by cannons smashing its walls. The ruins still stand near the Taos Pueblo.) Then the U.S. Army took over from the Spanish-Pueblo forces the bloody job of fighting Navajos, Apaches and Comanches. It proved to be the longest war in American history—lasting almost a half century.

The American Civil War brought a fourth flag to New Mexico. A Confederate column invading from Texas quickly captured federal forts in southern New Mexico, took Santa Fe, and then, met Union forces in the fateful battle of Glorieta Pass east of the capital. Partly through luck, a force of Colorado volunteers found and captured the entire supply train of the Confederate army in Apache Canyon. The Southerners withdrew, evacuated Santa Fe, and retreated back to Texas. In 1863, the Navajo threat was permanently broken by a midwinter scorched earth campaign. Colonel Kit Carson's troops slashed through the heartland of the Diné in northwestern New Mexico and northeastern Arizona, chopping down orchards, burning food supplies and destroying hogans. Most of the Navajos surrendered and subsequently were moved to a concentration camp-reservation at Fort Sumner. There, after hunger and disease thinned their ranks, they signed a peace treaty and were allowed to return to a reservation carved out of part of their homeland. Fighting out of strongholds in southern New Mexico mountains, the Apaches resisted for another quarter century, until Geronimo—the last war chief—surrendered to General Nelson Miles in 1886.

With the Kiowa-Comanche raiders penned on reservations in Oklahoma, the Navajos at peace, and the Apaches finally curbed, New Mexico's mining and cattle industries burgeoned. Millions of acres of almost virgin grassland were suddenly safe grazing for cattle. And the mountains, where the Apaches had made mining as dangerous as Russian roulette, were suddenly available for exploitation. There had been some gold and silver mining by the Spanish since early in the colonial period, and the Spanish had also opened the great copper deposits at Santa Rita. Now, prospectors swarmed into the mountains, and mining boomed. Ramshackle and rowdy camps sprouted in the Mogollons, the Black Range, the Jemez, the Sangre de Cristos, and elsewhere. Hillsboro, Kingston, Elizabethtown, Mogollon, Shakespeare, Golden, and a hundred other little towns flourished and died as the veins of ore were exhausted.

The mining boom was almost purely an Anglo-American affair, with little effect on the existing Spanish-Pueblo Indian cultures. The cattle boom was another matter.

On the plains country of New Mexico's eastside, it was largely a matter of filling a vacuum. The Kiowa-Comanches had dominated this buffalo grass country since the horse had given them their mobility. Now they were gone, and their empire was quickly seized by Texas ranchers and land-hungry immigrants from the ruined Confederacy. Animosity between Texans and the Spanish/Mexican cultures had long since become traditional. Along the buffalo plains feelings had been especially embittered by the practice of Spanish "comancheros" trading with the Indians and buying from them cattle and horses stolen in Texas. A brutal reprisal raid by Texas freebooters through northwestern New Mexico had worsened relations. Most of the few Spanish who had survived in the risky area along the Texas border were quickly dispossessed in actions which gave New Mexico some of its immense ranch spreads, and its old Spanish colonial families their "grandfather stories" of murder and injustice. In New Mexico, to call a man a "Tejano" (Texan) is still an insult.

In the Rio Grande Valley and the high plateau of northern New Mexico, history took another turn. The land grant system, one of the most practical devices of the Spanish colonial system, collapsed under the weight of Anglo-American occupation. The reasons were complex and the results—for the Spanish farmer-ranchers—were disastrous.

The Spanish Crown (later, the Viceroy in Mexico City and still later, Mexican authorities), had granted ownership of large tracts of land to the community of people who would use it. The Spaniards blocked out the land being used by the Indian Pueblos and set it aside for them. Other large tracts of land were issued to towns, villages and sometimes to families. Individuals might own a small homesite in the village in their own right, but the entire village shared the right to water, to grazing for their cattle, to timber and firewood. Many of these grants were described in vague terms, since the territory had not been surveyed. At the insistence of the Mexican government, a clause was written into the Treaty of Guadalupe Hidalgo whereby the United States guaranteed to honor the rights of the Pueblo Indians and the Spanish colonists under these grants. But honor proved to be a void. With the American occupation, the corrupt Mexican administration in Santa Fe was replaced by an equally corrupt U.S. administration. Under it, the pioneers began losing their land to the newcomers.

What may have been a stupid accident made it easier. A U.S. territorial governor, trying to make an office available in the Palace of the Governors for the arrival of a U.S. Attorney cleaned out the Spanish Colonial Archives. Bales of priceless documents dating back to the 16th Century were given away to be used as fuel. A deadline was set for the Spanish pioneers to file proof of their land ownership. It passed before many of them knew of it. Others discovered the documents they needed had been burned, or were in Mexico City or Spain. Some of this land was placed

in the public domain, eventually to become part of the National Forest. Much of it went into private ownership—through forced sales for unpaid property tax (an institution imported by the Anglo-Americans) by questionable "purchases" of land grants from a grant heir, with the transaction then approved in a corrupt court, by fraudulent surveys, and other devices. With the so-called "Santa Fe Ring" controlling the federal bureaucracy and the territorial courts, resistance was fruitless. Nevertheless, there sometimes was resistance.

For example after Lucien Maxwell sold part of his holdings, described as "two million acres, more or less," to a European syndicate, the farmers and ranchers living on this expanse (almost half the size of Massachusetts) fought to avoid eviction from their lands. After four years of intermittent bloodshed the syndicate finally prevailed, aided by the law and hired Pinkerton gunmen. In southwestern New Mexico, the so-called "American Valley War" flared when owners associated with the Santa Fe Ring blocked off access to water through fraudulent homestead claims. And in east-central New Mexico, where John Chisum's 150 square mile kingdom of grass stretched from Texas to the White Mountains, the struggle flared into the Lincoln County War, with Billy the Kid killing seven of his 21 victims as a gunman for the losing side. By the end of the 19th Century, little of the valuable land was left in the hands of the families who had tamed it. Thomas B. Catron, a former Confederate artillery captain who came to the territory fresh from a Union prisoner of war camp, and became a key figure in both the Santa Fe Ring and territorial politics, had become America's largest land owner. By 1896, he controlled the 827,621 acre Mora Land Grant, the 584,-515 acre Tierra Amarilla Grant, and at least five other grants plus extensive holdings elsewhere.

The 20th Century brought only relatively slow change to New Mexico. By 1912, when it became the 47th state, its population had reached only 330,000, and its economy was still based on small farms, great ranches, and a mixed-bag of mining—most notably the old Spanish workings at Santa Rita now developed into the immense open-pit Chino Mine by Kennecott Copper, coal in the northwest, and potash in the southeast. Early in the new century, artists had discovered the clear air. An art colony flourished first at Taos and then at Santa Fe, attracting writers, bohemians, rich eccentrics and assorted hangers-on. World War II accelerated the change. Robert Oppenheimer had attended the little Los Alamos Boys School on the Parajito Plateau across the Rio Grande from Santa Fe. He remembered the empty isolation of the place when the time came to pick a site for building the atomic bomb. Thus the Manhattan Project was moved to Los Alamos. What was to be a small hidden laboratory grew to be a scientific city of 15,000. The supporting Sandia Base and Laboratories at Albuquerque caused that city's population to soar from 35,500 in 1940, to 96,815 in 1950, to 201,190 in 1960, to an estimated 280,000 in 1974. Discovery of the free world's largest uranium deposits in the Ambrosia Lakes area west of Mount Taylor added a new dimension to the mining economy in the 1950s. Petroleum development boomed in the southeast corner of the state, and discovery of the great natural gas deposits in the northwest brought additional growth. But there is a limit to this growth. People require water, and water in New Mexico is scarce. Those who love its loneliness thank God for that.

U. S. Highway 64 runs westward—an asphalt line drawn ruler-straight through the sagebrush flats of the Taos Plateau. Behind you, an afternoon thunderstorm is building a top-heavy white tower over the Taos Mountains. To the northwest, another cloud has formed over the conical peak of San Antonio Mountain. Thirty miles ahead, the worn down highlands of the ancient Brazos Range form a low, blue line. You drive through a wilderness of silver-grey sage, relieved here and there by clusters of juniper, or piñon, or a meadow where the sickle blades of gramma grass are blowing. Then, with breath-catching suddenness you are on the Rio Grande Gorge bridge. The bridge, second highest arch in the United States, soars 2,000 feet from rim to rim. From eight hundred feet below, the sound of the river drifts upward. Here the river is hurrying, pouring down an endless series of falls, rapids and narrows. Down among the slick black basalt boulders, the noise is loud and constant. But heard from the bridge, the voice of the river is muted by distance, inaudible when the breeze whines through the steel structures, and no more than a grumble when the breeze is stilled. It seems too small to have cut this great gorge and too small for its name. Yet it is the nation's second longest river, extending 1,885 miles from its headwaters in the San Juan Mountains to its mouth in the Gulf of Mexico, draining a half-million square miles of Colorado, New Mexico, Texas and Mexico. And it is the aorta of New Mexico—the principal carrier of the water upon which more than half of the state's citizens depend. Under this bridge the water is clear and cold, fresh from melted snowpacks. Its deep pools are famous as the habitat of trophy-sized brown trout, but the steep and risky climb down the black cliffs restricts the fishing to those with sure feet and strong lungs. The sun reaches the bottom of this narrow slot only at midday, when it reflects hot and bright from the water-polished basalt. At other times, this is a cool, dim world of foam and spray, dark pools, with the world of men closed off by the constant lulling roar of falling water and the towering cliffs.

From the Colorado border southward past its junction with the Red River canyon, the gorge has been declared one of America's "Wild Rivers" with its untouched character to be preserved. Below this junction, at the place where Taos Creek pours its cold contribution into the river, the Rio Grande assumes another of its many characters. Here it is still clear, but the canyon widens and access is easier. Past the old village of Pilar, it tumbles over another series of milder rapids, popular with white water rafters. (The death toll among them has averaged about one per year.) The gorge has become the Rio Grande Canyon, and at Velarde, the wild river is subjected to its first

bridle. A diversion dam detours part of its water through the fields of the village.

New Mexico 68, which has followed the canyon much of the way from Taos into the Española Valley, skirts the old community on a hillside. The passerby looks down, in a sense, on the Spanish Colonial past. The tidy, compact village is a patchwork of apple, peach and cherry orchards, garden-sized fields of corn and chili, well-tended irrigation ditches, modest adobe homes—many tin-roofed here because of the snow. Draw a 100-mile circle around this village and you have the heart of what remains of America's Spanish Colonial culture. Truchas, Cundiyo, Chimayo, Santa Cruz, Talpa, Ranchos de Taos, Peñasco, Arroyo Seco, Arroyo Hondo, Rio Sarco and Ojo Sarco, Cordova, and Canjilon, Tierra Amarilla, El Valle, Llano, Rodarte—humble villages with proud names which once lined the northern frontier of the Spanish Empire. Each different and yet all alike. Most of them dating from the 18th Century—some from the 17th and some from the 19th—and all bypassed by the 20th. They are adobe villages, the color of the earth, peaked roofs against the high country snow or flat in valleys—and often sprouting weeds from their earthen insulation. In their way, Truchas and Las Trampas are typical. They were both built early in the 18th Century to guard Sangre de Cristo mountain passes against the marauding Comanches. Truchas is a double line of adobe houses lining a windy cliff edge under the Truchas Peaks and Las Trampas is a hollow square in the narrow valley of Rito las Trampas. They were there when George Washington was born. Truchas was founded by two families and Trampas by a man named Juan de Arguello. Arguello was 77 years old and a battle-scarred veteran of a long life of frontier wars when he led his sons-in-law and their families from Santa Fe to establish this lonely and dangerous new outpost. The chronicles report that when he was 99 he walked over the mountains to the Peñasco Valley to ask donations for the village chapel. He died at 117. With the U. S. occupation, the village lost all its communal grazing lands. But Las Trampas lives on, terribly poor, and terribly proud of its church which is a lovely and priceless example of Spanish-Colonial architecture. If you understand Juan de Arguello you can understand how a few hundred Spanish held this immense territory and why New Mexico Spanish-Americans are rooted to these northern mountains.

Below Velarde, the Rio Grande canyon opens into the Española Valley. The river is wider here, and slower moving, its banks now shaded by the cottonwoods. In the late autumn, they make it a ribbon of bright yellow all the way to Mexico. Here it irrigates the fields of the San Juan, Santa Clara and San Ildefonso Indians and roads through the last of its rapids in White Rock Canyon, now orange with the silt of the Rio Chama. It funnels between the Santa Fe Plateau and the Parajito Plateau, pouring past the mouths of the great canyons where many of the Pueblo Indians had their ancestral homes, and drops into the Santo Domingo Valley. Where the Pueblos of Santo Domingo and Cochiti have their reservations, the river is blocked by the Cochiti

Dam, one of the world's largest earthen structures. This dam will collect silt and control floods. But at this level, the river has already been taken firmly in hand by the Bureau of Reclamation's Middle Rio Grande Irrigation District. At Albuquerque, where it waters a widening expanse of orchards and alfalfa fields, its bed is usually dry sand by mid-summer—its flow diverted into canals. The district stretches more than 100 miles through central New Mexico —ending below the village of San Antonio. There the Rio Grande is sluggish, wandering through the San Marcial marshes in a stretch of country that man has never quite managed to tame.

In a way totally different than the noisy bottom of the Rio Grande Gorge, this stretch of river also offers escape from man. Here the generous Rio Grande withdraws its hospitality and cuts through barren country. The valley itself is more narrow and marshy than is true up river. To the west are the Coyote Hills, carpeted with bunchgrass, cactus and creosote bush. Behind them lie the San Mateo Mountains and behind the mountains the vastness of the Plains of San Agustin. East of the river, the Jornada del-Muerto, the stony, waterless plain which the Spanish feared, fills a 20-mile gap amid the valley and dark shape of the Oscura Mountains. The emptiness of this landscape is certified by what lies beyond this ridge. Trinity Site. The place picked for detonation of the first atomic bomb.

A community of Piro Indians tried this country, leaving a ruined pueblo to testify to their failure. The Spanish tried, and left only dots on the provincial maps. San Marcial, the settlement which gave its name to the marshes here, was wiped out twice by Rio Grande floods and permanently erased. Anglo-American latecomers established Clyde. A flood removed it. The valley was given, in name, to Antonio Sandoval—the final land grant before American occupation. But it belonged to whoever was strong enough to hold it—and foolish enough to try. It's called Bosque del Apache because their raiding parties used its shady cottonwood groves for rest and recuperation. Then John Chisum took it as part of his cattle empire. And finally, during the Great Depression, it fell into federal hands, and became a wilderness area and the Bosque del Apache National Wildlife Refuge. It is the winter home for perhaps half a million birds and—except for the high mountain species—the entire index of Southwestern mammals.

The four lanes of Interstate 25, southbound from Albuquerque to El Paso, leave the valley at Socorro and skirt through the foothills. Along the river there is only the narrow, abandoned pavement of what once was U. S. 85. Now the grass eats at the road's edges and sprouts through its cracks. If you stand beside your car here at dawn on a winter morning, and listen, and look, you can recapture how it was when the Apaches gave this place its name. The musical murmur on the still air is the conversation of birds—morning talk of tens of thousands of waterfowl, the odd fluting of sandhill cranes, the shrill note of red-winged blackbirds, and blended sounds of scores of other species. And then, about when the rim of the sun has put a bright red glow behind the Oscuras, there is the sound of wings. The snow geese are usually first, rising off the marsh ponds to fly upstream for their morning feeding. They swing to the west, a cloud of wings rising above the cottonwoods—not a swarming, disorderly blackbird rabble, but a kaleidoscope of a hundred shifting-but-orderly goose formations. Now the sunlight catches them, fifteen thousand great white birds sweeping past the gray velvet of the Coyote Hills, turning toward you. Then the sky overhead is filled with the clamor of an infinity of geese. You have looked through time and seen what America has lost.

Below the Bosque the river pours into Elephant Butte Reservoir—the long lake which waters the canals of Elephant Butte irrigation district. From here to its junction with the Texas-Mexican border, the river is simply a feeding system for part of America's most productive agricultural system. It grows long fiber cotton, onions, lettuce, and crops as varied as geese and pecans. In the lower valley, the land is as tamed, lush and ordered as anywhere in the nation. But 75 miles to the east, across the Organ Mountains, something called Lake Lucero has produced White Sands desert and comes as close as our continent can to total lifelessness. The opposite extreme of New Mexico's vertical climatic spectrum—the ice and granite ridges high above timberline, give an illusion of deadness. Even in August the air is frigid there, and nothing seems to grow or move. But the worn stone is stained with lichens, looking like gray scars, or blue velvet, or black stains depending on the variety, but nonetheless alive. And between the cracks, where freezing has produced a seedbed, every sunny place has its alpine sunflowers, or moss campion, or the tiny high-altitude gentians. The tough gray cold-climate grass is almost everywhere and, if you're patient, you'll see a goshawk against the dark sky and, far below at the upper fringes of forest, the blue-black flash of the stellar jay.

Northeast of Lake Lucero the illusion takes a totally different form and comes much closer to the truth. It's best to visit on a still winter day. You have driven down the Tularosa Basin, with the snowcapped Sacramentos looming to your left and to your right, at the very bottom of the valley, mile after mile of the tortured black lava flow which New Mexicans call malpais (bad country). Now, far to the south, between you and the San Andres-Organ mountain chain, you see White Sands, a long white, shimmering line. Fifteen miles beyond the irrigated agricultural oasis of Alamogordo, Highway 70, angling southwestward toward its pass through the Organs, intersects with this whiteness. A National Park Service visitors' center unmanned on this wintery evening, stands beside the highway. Past it, an access road leads westward over the alkali flats. And then the sands close around you. At the edges, some plants resist—saltbrush and iodine bush, skunkbush sumac, soap tree yucca and rubber pennyroyal—all species of incredible durability. But within moments, you inhabit a landscape of undulating white, surrounded by great dunes—some as high as 30 feet—of granulated gypsum crystals. You are in a landscape as dead and as pure as Antarctica.

There is nothing quite like it on the face of the earth. The name, White Sands, is misleading. This desert is not formed of sand. These dunes are born of water sweeping through the slopes of the surrounding mountains, eating away gypsum deposits and carrying this chemical in solution into the ten-mile long "playa" called Lake Lucero. Here the desert sun burns away the moisture, leaving sheets of dried gypsum crystals. These are eroded by the southwesterly wind. For hundreds of thousands of years this partnership of rain, sun and wind have moved the sands northeastward in a sheet which now covers 270 square miles.

When the air moves, the dunes march with infinite slowness. The crystals are carved out of their hard-packed southwestern slopes, pushed toward the soft summit, and rolled, finally, down the dune face a trillion-billion strong. They engulf the Park Service road and the skeleton of yucca, and whatever else lies in their path in an endless slow motion surf.

By its nature, desert seems to resist the idea of time. Its leafless spiny, sword-blade life ignores the cycle of seasons. Desert plants produce their brief explosion of flowers with more response to rare rainstorms than to any imagined seasonal fecundity. Spring brings only the arid wind and the dust devils hurrying aimlessly over a landscape of gray and brown and muted reds. (Over the White Sands, even these dust devils change. Instead of weightless dust, the spiralling winds pick up the heavy whiteness and hang almost motionless—glittering ropes connecting dunes and sky.) Within the Sands, this desert illusion of timelessness is intensified. On a windless winter afternoon here, the very planet seems dead. The silence is as pure as the crystals on which you stand. To the west, the Organs form an implausible ragged line against the sunset. To the northwest, the reflected light reddens the Sacramentos and highlights the snowpack on Sierra Blanca. The nearest fellow human is a long day's walk away.

Of course, there is more than this. There is the wind hooting through those odd volcanic walls which form miles-long rays from the base of the Shiprock. (A thousand feet overhead, among the crags of the monolith, Monster Slayer tricked the Winged Monster and killed it, and taught its offspring to be eagles. Thus was this area made safe for Navajos.) There is the old stone village of Zuni on Shalako night—playing host to the towering Messenger Birds and the Council of the Gods and feeding 3000 curious visitors on mutton stew and canned peaches. And Santa Fe under fresh snow—its ancient narrow streets looking like nothing else in America. And Aspen Basin when the leaves are falling from a thousand stark-white trunks—vertical lines that connect yellow floor with yellow ceiling. And the canyons of the Parajito Plateau where you still find Keresan magic scratched into the stone.

New Mexico is all of this, and a great deal more.

Temple of the Sun, Carlsbad Caverns National Park.

Rocky Mountain Bighorn Sheep, Pecos Wilderness
in May. Right: Sandia Peak view south along 10,600
foot alpine crest.

The Sandia Range is unique. Located on Albuquerque's edge it is a sublime haven for release of urban energy to the skier, hiker, and sightseer. The all year tramway ride lends spectacular vistas. Left: Ice tufts coat the autumn grasses along rim after October storm.

Winter day above the clouds on Sandia Peak with
Albuquerque glinting below. Left: Pennsylvanian
limestone crest and wind-flagged Limber pine.

Nightfall over Albuquerque. Left: Yucca stalks
silently outlined in a pre-dawn sky. Following pages a
great flotilla of cumulus parade a summer's
sky above the Tularosa Basin.

April Cherry blossoms in Old Town Albuquerque.
Right: On campus, University of New Mexico
at Albuquerque.

Corn, staple of the Pueblo diet drying on a door frame.
Right: Cloud-strung sky dwarfs church at Isleta Pueblo.

Passing summer shower veils the Mountains of Solitude,
Organ Mountains. Left: Nature's geometric design unfolds
in growing century plant, Rio Grande Valley.

Honey mesquite bloom, Rio Grande Valley.

Cooling aftermath of summer's thunderstorm,
Organ Mountains.

Cracking facade, Mogollon. One of remaining
buildings of a once-prosperous gold and silver mining
camp. Left: Memory of a booming past, Silver Creek
Canyon, Mogollon.

The Rio Grande River meanders along north of
Las Cruces. Right: The great silence, isolated volcanic
forms lend loneliness to the landscape, a lost sense
of proportion wildly exciting the imagination.

Home of the Ancients. Ruins of a desert people
crouch low in natural caves along the upper Gila River.
Left: Visitors today imagine how these Indians may
have lived, Gila Cliff Dwelling National Monument.

Santos, mural of the Saints, Las Trampas. Left: Universal
silence, an isolated butte stands in solemn testimony to the
loneliness of the New Mexico landscape, Cooks Range.

Fading storm over autumn cottonwoods in Taos. Left:
Horses in Cabresto Canyon. Following pages: Mingling of
the sun and earth spirits, sun descends behind the
San Andres Mountains, White Sands National Monument.

83

Ristras of chili drying in sun, Velarde.

Sunday services, Santuario de Chimayo.

Old Mike dwarfs ranch in Moreno Valley, Sangre de Cristo Range. Left: Cottonwood leaves at their turning in Fernando de Taos Canyon, Sangre de Cristo.

Winter image, village of Las Truchas and Truchas Peaks,
Sangre de Cristo Range. Right: Caretaker and guide.
Church in Las Trampas, a priceless example of Spanish
Colonial architecture along the high road to Taos.

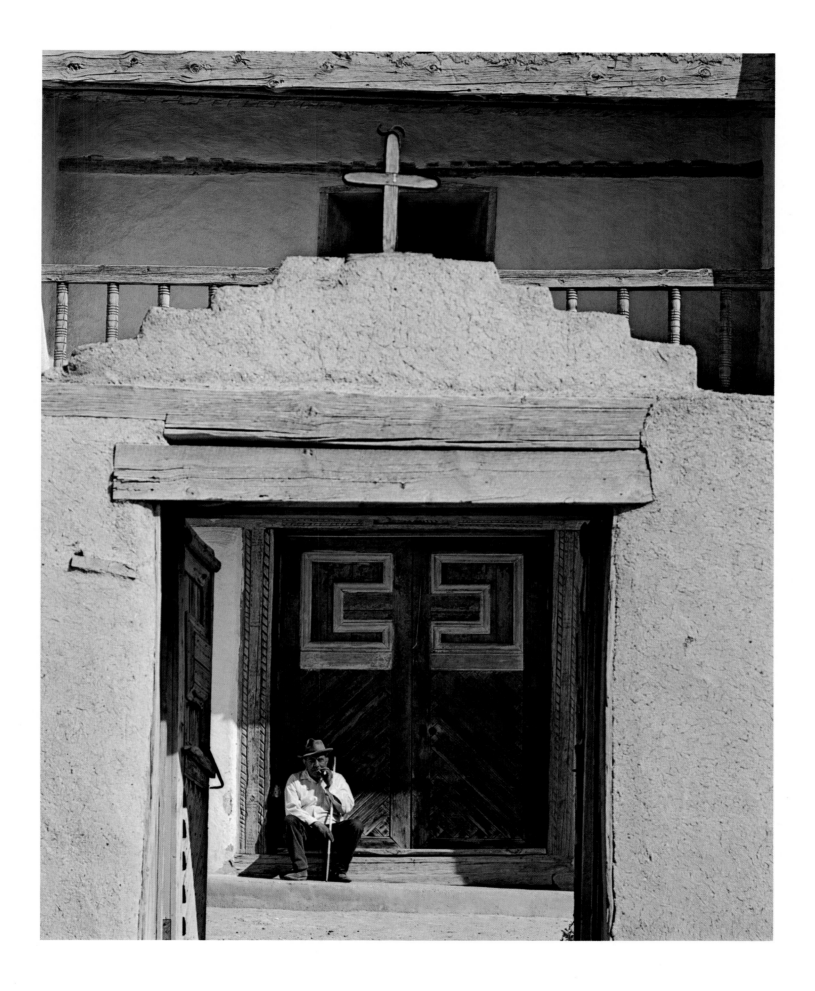

Church at Las Trampas. Left: Santos in church at Las Trampas. Village along the Rito Las Trampas was founded by 77 year old Juan de Arguello who led his sons-in-law with their families from Santa Fe.

Farmer raking hay in Mora Valley under tawny
thunderheads on the Rincon Range. Right: Maturing hay
crop nears harvest time in Peñasco on high road to Taos.

Above left: Tesuque creek cascades through dense
evergreen forest, Santa Fe National Forest. Above right:
Moss drapery on white fir in Palo Flechado Pass.
Left: Ranch spread near Angel Fire, Cimarron Range.

In the Latir Lakes country. Above right: A noonday sun on fir trees lining Latir Lake Number 3. Above left: Mule deer below Latir Peak. Left: Roaring spring-flow of cascade between Latir Lakes.

Kayak running in white water of the wild Rio Grande River as it pours through a series of falls, rapids and narrows in its black basalt gorge. Left: Melting snow drifts high in the Pecos Wilderness.

Rio de Trampas, Pecos Wilderness. Left: Sheep's Head
holds an icy cloud to its leeside, Truchas Peaks.

Flush of morning sunburst along the icy Rio Grande
River near Española. Left: Frosted salt cedar at base of
Shiprock in Navajo land.

Flight of Snow Geese in Bosque del Apache Migratory
Bird Refuge along the Rio Grande. Left: Volcanic rims of
the Rio Grande hold the nation's second longest
river in their tawny depths.

Wild Rio Grande River gorge, in area of Big Arsenic
Springs. At right: Refreshing flow of clear drinking water
gurgles between basalt boulders in a large series
of springs at Big Arsenic.

Skier in deep powder at Taos Ski Valley. Left: Snow moguls in Hondo creek. Following pages: Aspen boles with firs, Hondo Canyon in January, Sangre de Cristo.

In 1882 the discovery of coal fired this modest town
of Madrid along the Ortiz Mountains. Identical company
houses line quiet main street, the mill closed and relics
lay strewn around in a scene of dust and memory.

Battle shield figures on volcanics, Galisteo Basin.
Left: Mission church and pueblo ruins, Pecos National Monument.

Cristo Rey Church silhouette in Santa Fe.

North Chapel interior, St. Francis Cathedral, Santa Fe.

Dynamic artistry of Chicano mural, Santa Fe.
Right: Bell towers, San Miguel Mission—nation's oldest
mission church and a national historic landmark.

126

17th century Franciscan mission ruins silhouette against a dawn sky at Quarai State Monument. Left: Stark ruins of isolated 17th century church San Buenaventura above walls of Pueblo de las Humanas, Gran Quivira National Monument.

Cottonwoods dwarf Spanish mission ruins at Quarai.
Left: Sunburst in autumn-robed cottonwood in Cabresto
Canyon, Sangre de Cristo Range. Following pages:
Electrical storm ferments above farm near Fort Sumner.

Cattle browsing in field near Roswell along the fertile
Pecos River. Left: Tumbleweeds drape fence, Rio Grande
River Valley near Las Cruces.

Pecos River in San Miguel County. Right above:
Tularosa Valley corral and Malpais lava flow below 12,000
foot Sierra Blanca. Lower: Greater sandhill cranes,
Bosque del Apache National Wildlife Refuge.

137

Timeless forms—bread ovens and adobe structure, San Ildefonso Pueblo. Left: Turquoise pendant. Like a piece of fallen sky, precious stone is state gem.

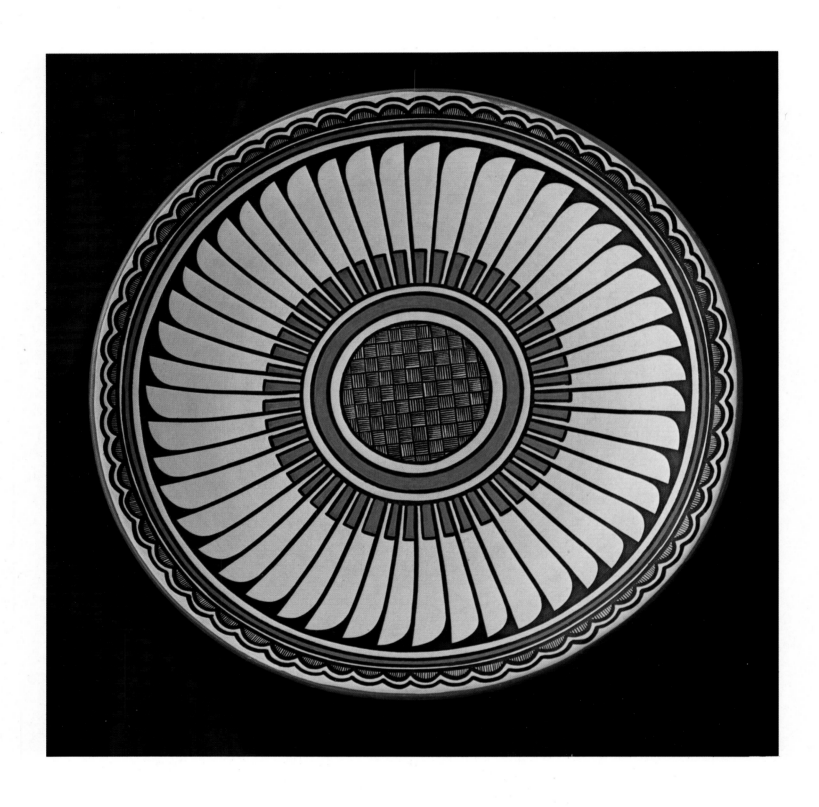

San Ildefonso Pueblo contemporary pottery. Polychrome
olla by Maria and Julian Martinez. Left: Polychrome platter
by Maria and her son Popovi Da.

Deer Dancers, San Ildefonso Pueblo. Painting at
Museum of Fine Arts, Santa Fe. Left: Silence of daylong
noon casts its eternal spell on San Ildefonso Pueblo.

Sun impressions, sunflower, Manzano Mountains.
Left: The setting sun loses itself in silhouette of isolated
butte, Cerrillos Hills.

Bread oven and dwellings in the north plaza of Taos
Pueblo. Right: Ceremonial kiva, Pueblo of Picuris.

Above: Prairie dog. Below: Primrose.
Right: Alchemy of sun and earth above Conchas Reservoir.

At once massive and delicate—Mission Saint Francis
of Assisi in Ranchos de Taos. Left: Taos Mountains dwarf
village of Ranchos de Taos.

Winter in Taos Pueblo—south plaza dwellings
across the Rio Taos. Left: Bread oven and main structures
of north plaza.

Autumn's gentle advance, Rito de los Frijoles,
Bandelier National Monument. Left: Aspen grove below
13,151 foot Wheeler Peak, New Mexico's highest.

Elizabethtown—fragments of bygone dreams in
Moreno Valley. Lone cross in E Town graveyard. Left:
Ruins of Mutz Hotel, once part of a rich gold mining center.

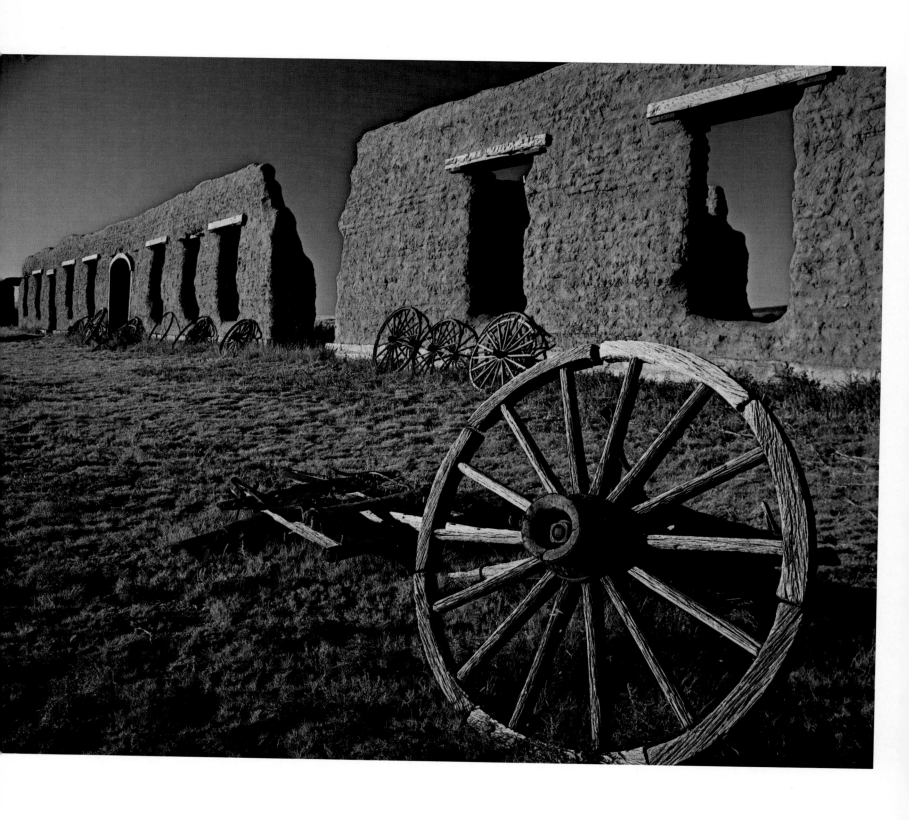

Post corral, Fort Union National Monument along Santa Fe
trail. Right: Rio Chama at Abiquiu, Jemez Mountains.

Summer flow of Jemez Falls in travertine formations.

Ruins of 17th century mission complex San Jose
de los Jemez at Jemez Springs, founded in 1621.

Herds of sheep graze summer pastures in high forests
above Tierra Amarilla. Left: Autumn flushes aspen groves
above the sheer Precambrian Brazos Peak. Following
pages: Campo Santo and Brazos cliffs, Tierra Amarilla.

Upper Falls, Frijoles Canyon, Bandelier National Monument.

High meadow blooms after summer rains, Moreno Valley.

Longhouse ruin, Frijoles Canyon, Bandelier National
Monument. Right: Tent rocks in the Jemez Mountains.

Above: Volcanic rim of Pajarito Plateau, Cerrillos
Hills beyond. Below: Pictographs in Painted Cave.

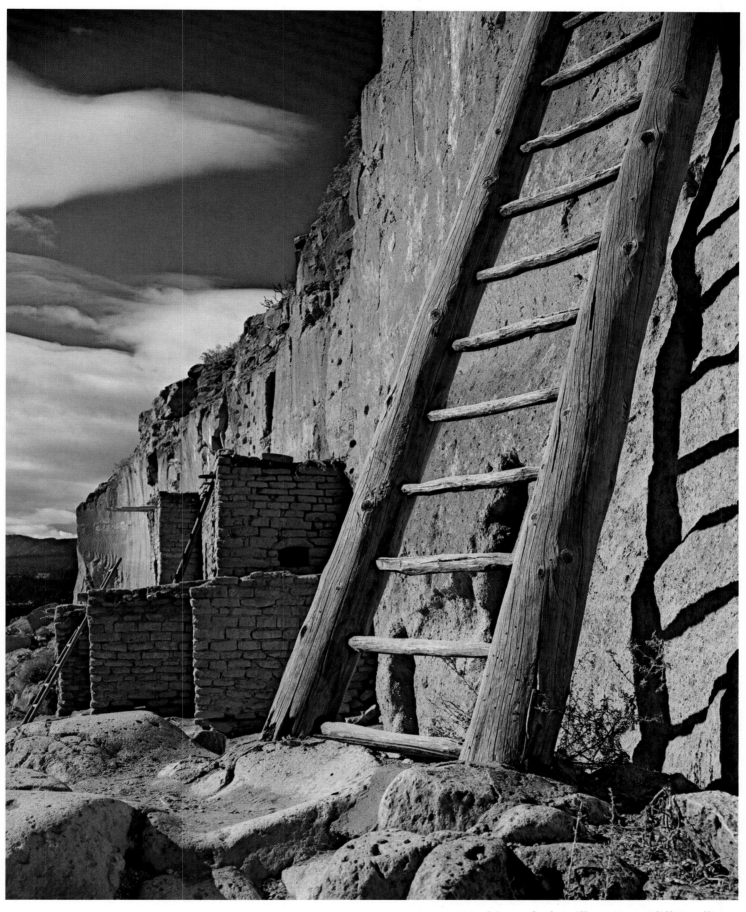

Ladder and talus village, Puye Cliff Dwellings.

Gypsum dunes of White Sands National Monument.
Crest of wavelike dune. Left: Yucca stalk momentarily
anchors gypsum grains in a constant procession
of changing dunes.

Undulating landscape of White Sands National Monument.
Left: Timeless ribbon of flow, Galisteo creek.

Above: Rim view of D shaped Pueblo Bonito.
Below: Kiva and walls, Chettro Kettle, Chaco Canyon
National Monument.

Interior communal doorways, Aztec National Monument.

Evening pastels, White Sands National Monument. Left:
The Spire and Razorback etch a jagged skyline in the
Organ Mountains east of Las Cruces. Following pages:
Chinese Theater, Carlsbad Caverns National Park.

179

Faded memories of gold and silver. Left: Victorian frame house at White Oaks. Right: Hoyle's Castle. Far right: Sunrise explodes in spray of Mountain Mahogany, Guadalupe Mountains.

Wintering home for migratory waterfowl, Bosque
del Apache National Wildlife Refuge. Snow geese in flight
from grain fields where they feed. Left: Reeds in design,
pool along Rio Grande River at San Antonio.

Isolated cabin graces ponderosa forest above Mora Valley,
Sangre de Cristo Range. Right: Asters and sunflowers in
summer profusion before Sierra Blanca.